Sanjeev Kapoor

Roti-Paranthe

In association with Alyona Kapoor

www.popularprakashan.com

Published by
POPULAR PRAKASHAN PVT. LTD.
301, Mahalaxmi Chambers
22, Bhulabhai Desai Road
Mumbai - 400 026
for Khana Khazana Publications Pvt. Ltd.

© 2011 Sanjeev Kapoor
First Published 2011
First Reprint 2014

WORLD RIGHTS RESERVED. The contents – all recipes, photographs and drawings are original and copyrighted. No portion of this book shall be reproduced, stored in a retrieval system or transmitted by any means, electronic, mechanical, photocopying, recording or otherwise, without the written permission of the author and the publisher.

(4421)
ISBN: 978-81-7991-673-5

Design: Anjali Sawant
Typesetting: Satyavan Rane
Photography: Bharat Bhirangi, Mangesh Parab, Satish Parab & Swapnil Naik

PRINTED IN INDIA
by Saurabh Printers Pvt. Ltd.
A-16, Sector 4, Noida

Contents

Author's Note — 5

No-Oil Multi-Grain Methi Chapati	6
Besan ki Masala Roti	7
Bakarkhani	11
Aam ka Parantha with Chhunda stuffing	13
Baby Bajra Roti	14
Mughlai Paranthe	15
Dalia aur Dal Paranthe	17
Bhature	18
Bidari Paranthe	21
Chawal ke Paranthe	22
Palak aur Paneer Paranthe	24
Luchi	26
Bikaneri Dal Paranthe	27
Dhania-Pudina Paranthe	31
Jawari Bhakri	33
Khaari Puri	34
Rice Wade	36
Jammu ka Aloo Anardana Paranthe	37
Khasta Roti	41
Kulche	42
Lachcha Paranthe	44
Lasun and Rice Thepla	46
Palak Paranthe	47
Koki	48

Methi-Makai Paranthe	51
Makki di Roti	53
Methi Paranthe	54
Aloo-Gobhi Paranthe	55
Mooli ke Paranthe	57
Moong Dal Puri	61
Mooli-Bajra Roti	63
Aloo-Anardana Kulche	65
Paneer Kulche	67
Sheermal	71
Paustik Bajre ki Roti	73
Rice Bhakri	74
Spicy Rajma Paranthe	75
Tikadia	77
Varqi Paranthe	81
Tandoori Pyaaz Kulche	83
Paneer aur Chawal Paranthe	85
Tandoori Roti	87
Teekhat Meethachi Puri	88
Missi Roti	89
Naan	91
Pudina Paranthe	93
Rajasthani Baati	95
Glossary	96

Author's Note

A traditional Indian spread is incomplete without roti or paranthe on the menu. Undoubtedly the cornerstones of Indian cuisine, these quintessential Indian flat breads are loaded with nutrition and flavour.

Roti and paranthe can make a meal by themselves or can be paired with a bhaji or gravy with equal ease.

With the goodness of wheat, jowar, bajra, rice, and other grains, they pack a nutritional punch. Make them part of your tiffin for work or school. They make a great snack option for those hunger pangs between meals. Leftovers also make a great stuffing for paranthe.

My new collection of vegetarian roti and paranthe will introduce you to a treasure of flavours and textures. Try the classic Makki di Roti, healthy Multi-Grain Methi Chapati, lusciously sweet Sheermal, and rustic Mooli Bajra Roti.

Turn up the heat under that tawa and roll out layers of flavour!

Happy Cooking!

Sanjeev Kapoor

No-Oil Multi-Grain Methi Chapati

½ cup gram flour

½ cup wholewheat flour

½ cup barley flour

1 cup fenugreek leaves, finely chopped

Salt to taste

¼ small cabbage, finely grated

½ cup yogurt

1 teaspoon red chilli powder

- Sift together the gram flour, wheat flour and barley flour and salt.
- Mix together the fenugreek and cabbage and mix into the flour mixture. Add the yogurt, chilli powder and water, a little at a time, to make a medium soft dough. Knead well.
- Cover with a damp cloth and set aside for about fifteen minutes.
- Divide the dough into eight to ten equal portions, and shape into balls. Roll out each ball into a five to six-inch *chapati*.
- Heat a non-stick *tawa* till moderately hot. Place *chapati* on the *tawa* and cook on one side for about half a minute.
- Flip it over and cook the other side. Lower the heat and cook on both sides till light brown. Serve hot.

Besan Ki Masala Roti

Roti

1 cup gram flour

½ cup wholewheat flour

Salt to taste

2 tablespoons pure ghee + for shallow-frying

Filling

1½ teaspoons cumin powder

½ teaspoon coriander powder

¼ teaspoon turmeric powder

1 green chilli, chopped

Salt to taste

½ teaspoon dried mango powder

½ teaspoon red chilli powder

1½ tablespoons pure ghee

- Combine all the ingredients for the filling in a small bowl. Set aside.
- Combine all the ingredients for the *roti* and knead into a soft dough using water as required.
- Divide the dough into eight portions and shape into balls.
- Roll out each ball into a four-inch disc and place one-fourth of the *masala* filling on it.

- Fold in half and then again in half to make a triangle. Roll out to make a triangular *roti*.
- Heat a non-stick *tawa* and fry each *roti* with a little ghee till both sides are golden brown.
- Spread a little ghee on the *roti* and press it gently between your palms.
- Serve hot.

Bakarkhani

2 cups refined flour

½ teaspoon baking powder

Salt to taste

¾ cup milk

2½ teaspoons sugar

1 tablespoon fresh yeast, crumbled

12-14 raisins, optional

1 tablespoon *chironji*

1 teaspoon screw pine essence

5 tablespoons pure ghee

10 almonds, blanched, peeled and sliced

- Heat the milk and add the sugar; stir till the sugar dissolves. Dissolve the fresh yeast in a quarter cup of warm water and set aside. Soak the raisins and *chironji* in half a cup of warm water for five minutes, drain and set aside.

- Sift together the refined flour, baking powder and salt. Make a well in the centre and add the sweetened milk, a few drops of screw pine essence and the yeast; gradually mix into a soft dough. Cover with a damp cloth and set aside for ten minutes.

- Gradually incorporate three tablespoons of melted ghee into the dough. Add the almonds, raisins and *chironji*. Knead once again, cover and leave to stand in a warm place for thirty minutes to rise.

- Divide the risen dough into eight equal portions, shape into balls, cover and set aside for ten minutes.
- Preheat an oven to 240°C/475°F/Gas Mark 9.
- Flatten the balls of dough and roll them out into five-inch rounds. Prick the surface of each one with a fork and arrange on a baking tray. Bake for ten to twelve minutes.
- Remove from the oven, brush with ghee and serve hot.

Note: *You need not grease the baking tray as the bakarkhani will release enough fat while baking. Do not use very hot water to dissolve yeast. The water should be lukewarm.*

Aam Ka Parantha With Chhunda Stuffing

2 cups wholewheat flour + for dusting

Salt to taste

½ cup mango pulp

2 tablespoons oil + for deep-frying

1 cup *chhunda*

- Make a dough with wheat flour, salt, mango pulp and two tablespoons of oil. Divide into eight equal portions.
- Dust each ball of dough with flour and roll out into a small *roti*. Brush with a little oil and sprinkle with a little flour.
- Place a tablespoon of *chhunda* at one end of the *roti* and roll into a cylinder.
- Fold in the two ends and press lightly. Cover and leave the rolls to rest for a while.
- Dust each roll with a little flour and gently roll out again into squares. Shake off excess flour.
- Heat a non-stick *tawa*. Place each *parantha* on it and cook both sides on medium heat.
- Drizzle some oil around the edges and cook till both sides are golden and crisp.
- Serve hot with *chhunda*.

Chef's Tip: *Chhunda* is a sweet-sour pickle made of grated unripe green mangoes. A popular Gujarati accompaniment.

Baby Bajra Roti

2 cups millet (*bajra*) flour

Salt to taste

4 tablespoons white butter (optional)

- Heat two or three cups of water in a non-stick pan till lukewarm.
- Combine one-fourth of the flour and salt to taste, and knead with lukewarm water to make a semi-hard dough. Roll into a ball.
- Wet your hands and pat the ball of dough into a *roti*.
- Heat a non-stick *tawa* till moderately hot and place the *roti* on it.
- Cook on one side and flip over. Continue cooking till the *roti* puffs up.
- Remove from heat and serve hot with butter.
- Repeat the process to make the rest of the *roti*.

Mughlai Paranthe

1½ cups refined flour + for dusting

1½ cups wholewheat flour

¼ cup semolina

Salt to taste

6 tablespoons ghee + for shallow-frying

½ cup milk

- Mix together the refined flour, wholewheat flour and semolina.
- Add salt, two tablespoons of ghee and the milk and knead into a stiff dough. Cover and leave to rest for thirty minutes.
- Divide the dough into eight equal portions; roll in refined flour and set aside to rest again for ten minutes.
- Roll out each portion into a thin *chapati* and brush with ghee. Dust with some flour and fold in half. Brush a little more ghee, dust with flour and once again fold lengthways in half.
- Stretch and roll up into a spiral and then roll once again into a ball. Press lightly with your fingers and roll out into a *parantha*.

- Heat a non-stick *tawa* and place each *parantha* on it.
- Turn over after a minute and spread ghee on the cooked side. Turn again and spread ghee on the other side too.
- Shallow-fry till both sides are cooked and golden.
- Crush lightly between the palms of your hands and serve.

Dalia Aur Dal Paranthe

¾ cup cracked wheat

¼ cup whole green gram

1 cup wholewheat flour

Salt to taste

1 inch ginger, finely grated

½ cup chopped fresh coriander

1-2 medium green chillies, finely chopped

2 teaspoons oil

- Combine the flour and the salt.
- Soak the green gram for about an hour. Pressure-cook the green gram and the cracked wheat in one and half cups of water until soft. Cool and mash the mixture.
- Add the flour and mix well. Add the grated ginger, chopped coriander, green chillies and water, if required, and knead into a soft, pliable dough. Cover the dough with a damp cloth and set aside for fifteen minutes.
- Divide the dough into eight to ten equal portions. Shape into balls and roll out each portion to a thin five to six-inch *parantha*.
- Brush a little oil on a hot non-stick *tawa* and place each *parantha* on it and cook on medium heat for half a minute on each side. Lower the heat and cook till both sides are slightly browned.

Bhature

2½ cups refined flour
½ teaspoon baking powder
A pinch of soda bicarbonate
½ cup yogurt
1 teaspoon salt
2 teaspoons powdered sugar
2 tablespoons oil + for deep-frying

- Sift together the refined flour, baking powder and soda bicarbonate.
- Mix the yogurt with salt and sugar. Add to the flour, with enough water and knead lightly to make a soft dough.
- Knead two tablespoons of oil into the dough. Cover the dough with a damp cloth and leave to rest for one hour.
- Divide the dough into sixteen equal portions. Roll into balls, cover with a damp cloth and leave to rise for ten minutes.
- Grease your palms with a little oil and flatten the balls. Roll out into five-inch round *bhature*.
- Heat the oil in a non-stick *kadai* and deep-fry the *bhature* on high heat till light brown on both sides. Drain on absorbent paper.
- Serve hot with *chhole*.

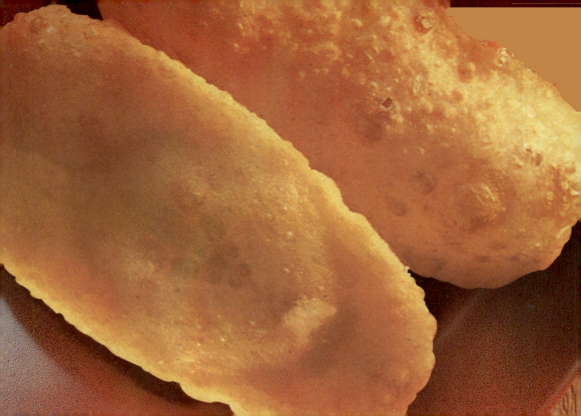

Bidari Paranthe

2 cups wholewheat flour

¾ cup refined flour

¼ cup semolina

Salt to taste

Oil for deep-frying

- Sift the wholewheat flour and refined flour together.
- Mix in the semolina, salt and three-fourth cup of water and knead into a stiff dough. Cover with a damp cloth for twenty minutes.
- Divide the dough into eight equal portions and shape into balls. Roll out each ball into a half-inch thick oval.
- Heat the oil in a non-stick *kadai* and deep-fry the *paranthe* one by one over high heat until puffed up and light golden brown.
- Drain on absorbent paper and serve hot.

Palak Aur Paneer Paranthe

8-10 large fresh spinach leaves
1½ cups wholewheat flour
½ cup refined flour
Salt to taste
1 teaspoon sesame seeds
Ghee for shallow-frying

Stuffing

300 grams cottage cheese, grated
3 green chillies, chopped
1 tablespoon chopped fresh coriander
1 small onion, chopped
1½ teaspoons *chaat masala*
Salt to taste

- Sift the wholewheat flour and refined flour with salt into a bowl and set aside.
- Blanch the spinach leaves in boiling water for one minute.
- Drain, squeeze out the excess water and blend to a thick purée in a blender.
- Add the spinach purée and sesame seeds to the flour and knead with enough water to make a soft dough.
- Cover the dough with a damp cloth and rest the dough for half an hour.
- For the stuffing, mix together the cottage cheese, green chillies, chopped coriander, onion, *chaat masala* and salt in a large bowl. Divide into eight equal portions.

- Knead the dough again and divide into eight equal portions. Shape into balls and press between your palms.
- Roll out each ball into a four-inch round and thin down the edges.
- Place one portion of the stuffing in the centre, gather the edges together and shape into a ball again. Roll out into a seven-inch round *parantha*.
- Heat a non-stick *tawa*. Place each *parantha* on it, turn over once and drizzle a little melted ghee around it.
- Turn it over again and spread a little more ghee on the other side. Cook till both sides are cooked.

- Remove from heat and allow to cool. Divide into eight portions and set aside.

- Divide the dough into eight portions and roll into balls.

- Shape each portion on your palm into a small *puri*; place a portion of stuffing in the centre, gather up the edges and shape into a ball again.

- Press each ball down lightly on a work surface. Roll out into a thin *parantha*, dusting with flour if required. The *parantha* should be as thin as a *papad*.

- Heat sufficient oil in a pan. Slide a *parantha* gently into the oil and shallow-fry till evenly golden brown on both sides.

- Drain on absorbent paper and serve hot.

Dhania-Pudina Paranthe

¼ cup finely chopped fresh coriander
¼ cup finely chopped fresh mint
2 cups wholewheat flour
Salt to taste
½ cup yogurt
2 teaspoons *chaat masala*

- Place the flour and salt in a bowl. Add the chopped coriander and mint, and knead into a soft dough with a little water.
- Cover and rest the dough for twenty to twenty-five minutes.
- Divide the dough into eight equal portions. Shape them into balls.
- Mix together the yogurt and *chaat masala*.
- Roll out each ball into a medium-sized *chapati*. Spread a tablespoon of the yogurt mixture over the *chapati*.
- Fold the *chapati* like a fan and roll the fan up to form a disc.
- Set aside for five minutes.

- Roll out each disc into a five to seven-inch round *parantha*. Cook on a hot non-stick *tawa* till both sides are lightly golden brown.

- Before serving, crush the *parantha* lightly between your palms to open out the layers.

Chef's Tip: If you are cooking these *paranthe* in a *tandoor*, apply a little water on the side that will stick to the *tandoor* wall.

Jawari Bhakri

2 cups sorghum (*jowar*) flour

Salt to taste

½ cup fresh white butter

- Mix together the flour and salt.
- Add enough water to make a soft dough; knead well.
- Divide the dough into eight equal portions. Shape each portion into a round ball. Roll out each portion of dough into a thin round (*bhakri*).
- Heat a non-stick *tawa* till moderately hot. Cook each *bhakri* on the *tawa* until one side is cooked.
- Sprinkle a little water on the *bhakri*, turn over and cook the other side till done.
- Serve hot with a dollop of fresh white butter.

Khaari Puri

- 1¾ cups wholewheat flour
- 2 tablespoons gram flour
- 2 tablespoons coriander powder
- 3 teaspoons red chilli powder
- ½ teaspoon *garam masala* powder
- Salt to taste
- 2 tablespoons pure ghee
- ½ teaspoon cumin seeds, crushed
- ½ teaspoon coriander seeds, crushed
- ¼ teaspoon turmeric powder
- 2 green chillies chopped
- Oil for deep-frying

- Combine the gram flour, coriander powder, chilli powder, *garam masala* powder and salt in a deep bowl.
- Heat the ghee in a non-stick *kadai*; add the cumin seeds, coriander seeds, turmeric powder and green chillies, and sauté for half a minute.
- Add the gram flour mixture and cook on medium heat till lightly browned and fragrant.
- Remove from heat and set aside to cool. Divide the mixture into eight portions.
- In a separate bowl, knead the flour and salt into a soft, smooth dough.
- Cover with a damp cloth and rest the dough for ten minutes.

- Divide the dough into eight portions. Roll out each portion into a three-inch disc and place a portion of the gram flour mixture in the centre.
- Gather the edges together and seal the dough. Roll into a ball and roll out again into a small *puri*.
- Heat sufficient oil in a non-stick *kadai* and deep-fry the *puri* till golden brown.
- Drain on absorbent paper. Serve hot.

Rice Wade

2 cups rice flour

2 tablespoons fennel seeds

1 tablespoon fenugreek seeds (*methi dana*)

Salt to taste

1 small onion, grated

Oil for deep-frying

- Boil one and a quarter cups of water with the fennel and fenugreek seeds for about five minutes to extract their flavour.
- Strain and reheat the water. Stir in the salt and rice flour and cook, stirring continuously, till the mixture comes together and leaves the sides of the pan.
- Transfer the dough to a bowl, add the grated onion and mix well.
- Grease your palms and divide the dough into twelve equal balls. Press each ball of dough between your palms to make a *wada*.
- Heat the oil in a non-stick *kadai* and deep-fry the *wade* till golden brown and cooked. Drain on absorbent paper and serve hot.

Chef's Tip: You can also shape the wade on greaseproof paper. Place a ball of dough between two sheets of greased greaseproof paper and flatten it with a rolling pin or your fingers. Remove the top sheet of paper and gently remove the *wada* from the bottom sheet and deep-fry.

Jammu Ka Aloo Anardana Paranthe

- 2 large potatoes, boiled, mashed
- 1 teaspoon pomegranate seeds, roasted and powdered
- 2 cups wholewheat flour
- Salt to taste
- 2 tablespoons milk
- 2 tablespoons yogurt
- 1 small onion, chopped
- ½ teaspoon red chilli powder
- 2 green chillies, chopped
- 1 teaspoon *chaat masala*
- 2 tablespoons chopped fresh coriander

- Place the wholewheat flour in a bowl, add the salt, milk, yogurt and sufficient water and knead into a soft dough.
- Cover with a damp cloth and set aside for fifteen minutes. Divide the dough into eight portions.
- Add the onion to the mashed potatoes along with salt, chilli powder, green chillies, roasted pomegranate powder, *chaat masala*, chopped coriander and salt, and mix well.
- Divide into eight portions. Roll out each portion of the dough into a small *puri*, place one portion of potato stuffing in the centre, gather in the edges and roll out into a ball. Roll out into a *parantha*.

- Heat a non-stick *tawa*. Place a *parantha* on it and roast for half a minute. Flip it over and dab some water on the top.
- Flip it over again and dab some water on the other side as well.
- Continue to roast till both the sides are evenly lightly browned.
- Serve hot.

Khasta Roti

1 cup refined flour

2 tablespoons semolina

Salt to taste

1 teaspoon sugar

4 tablespoons ghee

½ teaspoon carom seeds

- Dissolve the sugar and salt in half a cup of water.
- Mix together the refined flour, semolina, ghee, carom seeds, salt and sugar solution. Add sufficient water to make a stiff dough.
- Divide the dough into eight equal portions and shape into balls.
- Flatten each ball and roll out into a six-inch *roti*.
- Heat a non-stick *tawa* and roast each *roti* on both sides till crisp.
- Serve hot.

Kulche

2 cups refined flour

Salt to taste

¼ teaspoon soda bicarbonate

2 tablespoons yogurt

2 tablespoons milk

3 tablespoons oil

¾ teaspoon onion seeds

2 tablespoons butter

- Sift the flour with salt and soda bicarbonate. Gradually mix in the yogurt and milk.
- Add sufficient water to make a soft, smooth dough. Cover with a damp cloth and rest the dough for ten minutes.
- Add two tablespoons of oil and knead the dough well.
- Cover once again and set aside for at least one hour. Divide the dough into six to eight equal portions and shape into smooth balls.
- Place the balls on a lightly floured surface and roll out gently into four to five-inch rounds. Brush lightly with oil, sprinkle the onion seeds on top and press between your palms.

- Preheat an oven to 220°C/425°F/Gas Mark 7.
- Place the *kulche* on a greased baking tray and bake for about six to eight minutes.
- Brush the hot *kulche* with butter.
- Serve immediately.

Chef's Tip: Traditionally *kulche* are cooked in a *tandoor*.

Lachcha Paranthe

1½ cups wholewheat flour
½ cup refined flour
Salt to taste
6 tablespoons pure ghee
3 tablespoons milk
1 tablespoon sugar

- Sift both the flour and salt into a mixing bowl. Rub in one tablespoon of ghee with your fingertips.
- Warm the milk in a non-stick pan and dissolve the sugar in it.
- Add the mixture to the sifted flours and mix thoroughly. Add enough water and knead lightly to make a soft dough.
- Divide into four portions and shape into balls. Roll out each ball into a thin six to seven-inch round *roti*.
- Brush the entire surface of each *roti* with one tablespoon of melted ghee and dust with flour. Pleat the *roti* to make a number of folds.

- Roll up into a spiral. Press between your palms and set aside for five minutes. Roll out lightly into a six-inch *parantha*.
- Heat a non-stick *tawa*; cook each *parantha* on both sides on medium heat.
- Pour a little ghee all around and shallow-fry the *parantha* till both sides are golden brown.
- Lightly crush the *parantha* with your hands to separate the layers.
- Serve immediately.

Lasun And Rice Thepla

- 2 cups wholewheat flour
- 1 tablespoon garlic paste
- 2 tablespoons fresh green garlic, chopped (optional)
- 1 cup leftover cooked rice, mashed
- ½ teaspoon turmeric powder
- 1 teaspoon red chilli powder
- Salt to taste
- 2 tablespoons chopped fresh coriander
- 4 tablespoons oil + for shallow-frying

- Place the flour, garlic paste, green garlic, mashed rice, turmeric powder, chilli powder, salt and fresh coriander in a bowl.
- Mix in four tablespoons of oil and knead with enough water into a medium soft dough.
- Divide into twelve portions and roll each one out thinly into five-inch round *thepla*.
- Heat a non-stick *tawa* and cook the *thepla* on both sides drizzling a little oil around.
- Serve hot with pickle or yogurt.

Palak Paranthe

500 grams spinach leaves

1¼ cups wholewheat flour

3-4 green chillies, seeded and roughly chopped

Salt to taste

½ cup ghee

- Coarsely chop hundred grams spinach; blanch the rest and refresh in cold water.
- Purée the blanched spinach and the green chillies.
- Sift the wholewheat flour with the salt and make a soft dough with spinach purée, chopped spinach and water if needed.
- Cover with a damp cloth and set aside for thirty minutes.
- Divide into eight equal portions and shape into balls. Roll out each portion, brush with some ghee and fold in half.
- Fold again into a quarter. Roll out into six-inch triangles
- Heat a non-stick *tawa* and place each *parantha* on it. Turn it over and drizzle a little ghee around it.
- Turn over again and brush a little ghee on the other side as well. Cook till both sides are evenly cooked.
- Serve hot with the yogurt.

Roti-Paranthe

Koki

2½ cups wholewheat flour

2 small onions, roughly chopped

Salt to taste

2-3 green chillies, finely chopped

2 tablespoons fresh coriander, chopped

1 tablespoon ghee + for shallow-frying

4 tablespoons fresh cream

- Mix together the flour, onions, salt, green chillies, chopped coriander, one tablespoon of ghee and cream in a bowl.
- Add enough water to make a stiff dough. Cover and rest the dough for about fifteen minutes.
- Divide the dough into eight equal portions, larger in size than that needed to make a *parantha*. Pat with your fingers into a thick round.
- Heat a non-stick *tawa*, place the *koki* on it and cook on both sides. Brush with ghee and cook till both sides are light golden brown.
- Serve hot.

Methi-Makai Paranthe

- ½ cup fresh fenugreek leaves, chopped
- ½ cup sweetcorn kernels, boiled and crushed
- 2 cups wholewheat flour
- Salt to taste
- 4 tablespoons ghee
- 1 small onion, chopped
- 1 medium potato, boiled and mashed
- 2 tablespoons fresh coriander, chopped
- 2 green chillies, chopped
- ½ teaspoon carom seeds
- 1 tablespoon lemon juice

- Mix together the wholewheat flour and salt, and knead with enough water into a soft dough.
- Divide into eight equal portions and cover with a damp cloth for about fifteen minutes.
- Heat one tablespoon of ghee in a non-stick *kadai*; add the onion, corn and fenugreek leaves and sauté for a few minutes. Spread out on a plate to cool.
- Mix the sautéed mixture with the mashed potato. Add the chopped coriander, green chillies, carom seeds, lemon juice and salt, and mix well. Divide into eight equal portions.

- Roll out each portion of dough into a small *puri*, place a portion of stuffing in the centre, gather the edges together and roll into a ball.
- Roll out the ball into a five-inch round *parantha*.
- Heat a non-stick tawa, place each *parantha* on it and cook till light golden specks appear.
- Brush the top with a little ghee and turn it over.
- Cook the other side and brush with ghee. Serve hot.

Makki Di Roti

1½ cups cornmeal

¼ cup wholewheat flour, optional

Salt to taste

Fresh homemade white butter

- Add salt and wholewheat flour to the cornmeal and mix well. Add warm water and knead to make a medium soft dough. Divide into eight equal portions and shape into balls.
- Pat each ball between moistened palms to make a *roti* of medium thickness. Alternatively, roll out each ball between the folds of a greased plastic sheet.
- Heat a non-stick *tawa* and place a *roti* on it. Cook on moderate heat till one side is half-done.
- Turn over and spread some white butter over the surface. Turn over and spread some more butter on the other side. Cook till both sides are golden brown.
- Serve hot with a dollop of white butter.

Methi Paranthe

1 cup chopped fresh fenugreek

1 cup wholewheat flour

½ cup gram flour

Salt to taste

1 teaspoon red chilli powder

3 tablespoons ghee

½ cup yogurt

½ ripe banana, peeled and mashed

4 tablespoons oil

- Sift together the flour, gram flour, salt and chilli powder.
- Add the fresh fenugreek, ghee and yogurt, and mix well. Add the mashed banana and two tablespoons of oil, and knead into a stiff dough.
- Cover with a damp cloth and set aside for twenty minutes.
- Divide into eight equal portions and roll each one out into a five-inch round.
- Cook on a hot non-stick *tawa*, brushing both sides with a little oil, till cooked and light golden brown.

Chef's Tip: This dough does not need any water and the *parantha* can stay fresh for three or four days. It is the ideal food for long journeys.

Aloo-Gobhi Paranthe

3 medium potatoes, boiled, peeled and mashed

½ medium cauliflower, grated

3 cups wholewheat flour + for dusting

Salt to taste

2 tablespoons oil + for shallow-frying

2 tablespoons fresh coriander, chopped

3 green chillies, crushed

½ inch ginger, grated

½ teaspoon red chilli powder

- Place the flour into a deep bowl. Add the salt to taste and rub in two tablespoons of oil.
- Add water and knead well to make a stiff dough.
- Cover and rest the dough for fifteen to twenty minutes.
- Mix the potatoes and cauliflower. Add the chopped coriander, green chillies, ginger, chilli powder and salt to taste. Divide into eight equal portions.
- Divide the dough into eight equal portions and make small *peda* (flattened balls). Cover with a damp cloth and rest the dough again for five minutes.
- Flatten each ball by pressing it with your fingers so that the edges are thinner than the centre.

- Place one portion of potato-cauliflower mixture in the centre of the flattened dough, gather the edges together and shape again into a *peda*.
- Seal the edges completely so that the stuffing does not ooze out.
- Sprinkle a little flour on a smooth surface. Flatten the stuffed *peda* again, and roll each one out into a six-inch round *parantha*.
- Heat a non-stick *tawa*; place a *parantha* on it and cook on moderate heat for two minutes on either side.
- Spread half a tablespoon of oil on one side of the *parantha*, flip over and spread half a tablespoon of oil on the other side as well. Cook over low heat till both sides are golden brown. Serve hot with fresh yogurt or mango pickle.

Mooli Ke Paranthe

3 medium radishes with leaves
3 cups wholewheat flour + for dusting
Salt to taste
2 tablespoons ghee + for shallow-frying
½ teaspoon red chilli powder
¼ teaspoon carom seeds, crushed
2 green chillies, chopped
2 tablespoons chopped fresh coriander

- Grate the radish and finely chop the radish leaves. Squeeze out the juice from the grated radish. Reserve the radish and the juice separately.
- Mix together the wholewheat flour and salt in a bowl. Rub in two tablespoons of ghee with your fingertips.
- Add the reserved radish juice and knead into a soft dough, adding a little water if necessary. Cover with a damp cloth and rest the dough for fifteen minutes.
- Combine the grated radish, chopped leaves, chilli powder, carom seeds, green chillies and chopped coriander in a bowl. Divide the mixture into eight equal portions.

- Divide the dough into eight equal portions.
- Flatten each portion, making the edges thinner than the centre.
- Place a portion of the filling in the centre and sprinkle with salt.
- Gather the edges together and roll into a ball.
- Press the ball slightly to flatten, and roll out into a *parantha* on a greased and floured board or table.
- Heat a non-stick *tawa*. Place each *parantha* on the *tawa* and cook for one minute.
- Turn over and drizzle a little ghee over it. Turn over once again and drizzle a little ghee on the other side.
- Cook till both sides are golden and crisp on the outside.
- Serve hot.

Moong Dal Puri

½ cup skinless split green gram, soaked

1½ cups wholewheat flour

3 tablespoons oil + for deep-frying

1 teaspoon ginger paste

1 teaspoon red chilli powder

½ teaspoon coriander powder

¼ teaspoon cumin powder

¼ teaspoon *garam masala* powder

Salt to taste

- Drain and coarsely grind the green gram.
- Heat two tablespoons of oil in a non-stick pan. Add the ginger paste and sauté for half a minute on medium heat.
- Add the chilli powder, coriander powder, cumin powder and *garam masala* powder, and sauté for half a minute.
- Add the salt and ground gram, and sauté for three to four minutes. Set aside to cool.
- Place the wholewheat flour in a deep bowl. Add the salt, one tablespoon of oil and sufficient water and knead into a soft dough. Cover with a damp cloth and rest the dough for fifteen minutes.

- Divide both the dough and the stuffing into eight portions each. Take each portion of the dough in your palm and spread it slightly.
- Place a portion of stuffing in the centre, gather in the edges and roll into a ball. Roll out into a three-inch *puri*.
- Heat sufficient oil in a non-stick *kadai* and deep-fry the *puri*, one by one, till lightly browned.
- Drain on absorbent paper and serve hot with yogurt.

Mooli-Bajra Roti

3 medium radishes, grated
2 cups millet (*bajra*) flour + for dusting
Salt to taste
1 small onion, finely chopped
2 green chillies finely chopped
1 teaspoon red chilli powder
1 teaspoon ginger paste
1 teaspoon dried mango powder
½ teaspoon *garam masala* powder
2 tablespoons finely chopped coriander
Ghee for shallow-frying

- Mix some salt into the grated radish and set aside for half an hour. Squeeze tightly to remove excess moisture.
- In a deep bowl, mix the radish, millet flour, onion, green chillies, chilli powder, ginger paste, dried mango powder, *garam masala* powder, chopped coriander and salt thoroughly. Add sufficient warm water and knead into a dough.
- Divide the dough into eight equal portions and roll into balls. Lightly dust each ball with flour, place on a plastic sheet and pat with your fingers into a thick *roti*.
- Heat a non-stick *tawa* and place each *roti* on it. Cook for a while, then flip the *roti* over and drizzle some ghee all around.

- Flip the *roti* over again and drizzle some more ghee all round and cook till both the sides are cooked and golden brown.

- Serve hot with a dollop of ghee.

Chef's Tip: Do not rest the dough as the radish will release water and make the dough sticky.

Aloo-Anardana Kulche

2 medium potatoes, boiled and grated

1 teaspoon dried pomegranate seeds, roasted and coarsely powdered

2 cups refined flour

¼ teaspoon soda bicarbonate

Salt to taste

2 tablespoons yogurt

2 tablespoons milk

4 tablespoons olive oil

½ medium onion, chopped

¼ cup chopped fresh coriander

8-10 fresh mint leaves, chopped

2 green chillies, chopped

½ tablespoon red chilli powder

1 tablespoon roasted cumin powder

¾ teaspoon onion seeds

2 tablespoons extra-virgin olive oil

- Sift the refined flour with the soda bicarbonate and salt into a bowl.
- Gradually mix in the yogurt and milk. Add sufficient water to make a soft, smooth dough. Cover with a damp cloth and rest the dough for ten minutes.
- Add two tablespoons of olive oil and knead the dough well. Cover it once again and set aside for at least an hour.

- Divide the dough into six to eight equal portions and shape them into smooth balls.
- Preheat an oven to 220°C/425°F/Gas Mark 7. Grease a baking tray with a little olive oil.
- Mix together the potatoes, onion, chopped coriander, mint leaves, green chillies, dried pomegranate seed powder, chilli powder, roasted cumin powder and salt to taste.
- Divide the potato mixture into six to eight equal portions and set aside.
- Flatten a portion of dough, place a portion of the potato mixture in the centre and fold the edges over to form a ball.
- Place each stuffed ball on a lightly floured surface and roll gently into a four to five-inch disc.
- Brush lightly with a little of the remaining olive oil, sprinkle a few onion seeds on the surface and press lightly with your palm.
- Place the *kulcha* on the greased baking tray and bake in the preheated oven for about six to eight minutes.
- Brush the hot *kulcha* with extra-virgin olive oil and serve immediately.

Paneer Kulche

Dough
1 cup refined flour
1 cup wholewheat flour
½ teaspoon baking powder
¼ teaspoon soda bicarbonate
½ teaspoon salt
1 teaspoon sugar
½ cup milk
1 tablespoon yogurt
1 tablespoon olive oil/rice bran oil

Stuffing
200 grams cottage cheese, grated
2 green chillies, chopped
2 tablespoons chopped fresh coriander
Salt to taste

- Sift together the flour, baking powder, soda bicarbonate and salt into a bowl.
- Add the sugar, milk, yogurt and one-fourth cup of water. Knead well into a medium soft dough.
- Brush the oil on the dough, cover with a damp cloth and set aside for one hour.
- Divide the dough into four equal portions and shape into balls.
- Place the cottage cheese in a bowl. Add the green chillies, chopped coriander

and salt, and mix well. Divide into four equal portions.

- Preheat an oven to 180°C/350°F/Gas Mark 4.
- Place the dough balls on a lightly floured surface. Flatten them slightly.
- Place a portion of the cottage cheese stuffing in the centre of each one, gather the edges and seal.
- Cover with a damp cloth and rest for five minutes.
- Flatten each ball between your palms to make a nine-inch disc
- Place the *kulche* on a baking tray and bake in the preheated oven for about fifteen minutes. You can also cook them on a non-stick *tawa* till both sides are evenly cooked.
- Alternatively place the *kulcha* on a cushioned pad and stick onto the interior walls of a moderately hot *tandoor* and bake for three to four minutes.
- Serve hot.

Sheermal

2 cups refined flour

Salt to taste

2 teaspoons sugar

¾ cup + 3 tablespoons warm milk

A few saffron threads

2-3 drops of screw pine essence

¼ cup pure ghee

2 tablespoons butter + for greasing

- Sift the flour with salt.
- Dissolve the sugar in three-fourth cup of warm milk. Soak the saffron in three tablespoons of warm milk.
- Add the sweetened milk and two to three drops of screw pine essence to the sifted flour and mix well.
- Add one-eighth cup of water and knead into a soft dough. Cover with a damp cloth and set aside for ten minutes.
- Melt the ghee and add it to dough; mixing it in well.
- Knead again into a soft dough. Cover and rest the dough for ten minutes.
- Divide the dough into sixteen equal portions and shape into balls. Cover and set aside for ten minutes.

- Preheat an oven to 240°C/475°F/Gas Mark 9.
- Flatten the balls on a lightly floured surface and roll out each ball into six-inch rounds. Prick the entire surface with a fork.
- Grease a baking tray with the butter, arrange the discs on it and bake in the preheated oven for eight minutes.
- Remove, brush the *sheermal* with the saffron-flavoured milk and bake again for three to four minutes.
- Remove, brush with butter and serve immediately.

Paushtik Bajre Ki Roti

1 cup millet (*bajra*) flour
¼ cup wholewheat flour
Salt to taste
1 medium onion, grated
1 medium carrot, grated
2 green chillies, chopped
1 teaspoon carom seeds

- Sift together the millet flour, wholewheat flour, and salt. Add the grated onion, grated carrot, green chillies and carom seeds. Add water, a little at a time, and knead the mixture into a medium soft dough. Do not over handle the dough.

- Divide the dough into eight equal portions and shape into balls (*pede*). Wet your palms with water, take each portion of dough and pat it between your palms to make thin four or five-inch *roti*.

- Heat a non-stick *tawa* and place each *roti* on it. Cook one side for about half a minute over medium heat; flip the *roti* over and cook the other side. Lower heat and cook both sides till the *roti* is slightly browned. Serve hot.

Chef's Tip: It takes some practice, but you must try to make the *roti* as thin as possible.

Rice Bhakri

2 cups + ¼ cup rice lour

Salt to taste

Sesame seeds, as required

- Sift together two cups of rice lour and salt. Add enough warm water to make a soft dough.
- Divide the dough into four portions and shape into balls.
- Dust a *thali* or a table top with a little rice lour. Flatten each portion of the dough with your palm into a moderately thick *bhakri*.
- Heat a non-stick *tawa* till moderately hot and place a *bhakri* on it.
- Brush the top of the *bhakri* with water while it is cooking; turn it over and cook the other side as well, brushing the top with water.
- When almost cooked, sprinkle the sesame seeds on top. The *bhakri* should be soft and fluffy.

Spicy Rajma Paranthe

- ⅓ cup red kidney beans
- 1 cup wholewheat flour
- 2 tablespoons soya flour
- 1 teaspoon red chilli powder
- 3-4 green chillies, finely chopped
- ½ teaspoon dried pomegranate seeds, ground
- 8-10 mint leaves, finely chopped
- 2 tablespoons tomato purée
- Salt to taste
- 2 teaspoons oil

- Soak the kidney beans overnight, or for at least six hours. Pressure-cook in two cups of salted water till soft.
- Drain thoroughly, cool and mash well. Reserve the cooking liquid.
- Mix together the flour, soya flour, mashed kidney beans, chilli powder, green chillies, ground pomegranate seeds, chopped mint, tomato purée and salt to taste.
- Add the reserved cooking liquid, if necessary, and knead into a soft pliable dough. Cover with a damp cloth and set aside for fifteen minutes.
- Divide into eight to ten equal portions and shape into balls.

- Roll out each portion into five to six-inch rounds. Brush a little oil on a hot non-stick *tawa* and place each *parantha* on it.
- Cook on medium heat for half a minute on each side.
- Lower the heat and cook till both sides are slightly brown.
- Serve hot, with fresh yogurt.

Tikadia

1½ cups wholewheat flour
Salt to taste
6 tablespoons pure ghee + to serve
1 teaspoon roasted cumin seeds
½ teaspoon red chilli powder
1 medium onion, chopped
½ medium tomato, chopped
2 teaspoons chopped fresh coriander

- In a large bowl, combine the flour, salt and four tablespoons of ghee.
- Add sufficient water and knead to make a soft dough. Divide the dough into four equal portions.
- In a bowl, combine the cumin seeds, chilli powder, onion, tomato and chopped coriander. Divide the mixture into four portions.
- Roll out each portion of dough into a thick three-inch disc and brush a little ghee on it.
- Place a portion of the onion-tomato mixture in the centre.

- Sprinkle a little salt. Gather the edges together and seal. Press and roll out into a thick *roti*.
- Heat a non-stick *tawa* and cook the *roti* on medium heat till golden brown on both sides.
- Serve hot, topped with a dollop of ghee.

Varqi Paranthe

4 cups refined flour

1 cup milk

2½ teaspoons sugar

Salt to taste

¾ cup pure ghee + for shallow-frying

- Warm the milk slightly and dissolve the sugar in it.
- Sift the flour with the salt. Make a well in the centre of the flour; pour in the milk and about half a cup of water.
- Mix into the flour gradually and knead into a soft dough.
- Cover with a damp cloth and set aside for ten minutes.
- Melt the ghee and add two-thirds to the dough, incorporating it gradually; knead again. Cover the dough and set aside for ten minutes.
- Place the dough on a lightly-floured surface and flatten with a rolling pin into a rectangular shape.
- Brush one-fourth of the remaining ghee evenly over the rolled dough, dust with the flour, fold one end over two-third of the rectangle, and then fold the other end over it to make three folds.
- Cover and refrigerate for ten minutes. Repeat this process thrice.
- Roll the dough into a one-eighth-inch thick rectangle and cut out four-inch circles with a cutter.

- Make three crisscross evenly spaced incisions on the surface of each *parantha*.
- Place the *paranthe* on greaseproof paper and refrigerate until ready to cook.
- Heat a non-stick *tawa*; add the ghee and cook the *paranthe* over low heat until golden brown on both sides.
- Serve immediately.

Chef's Tip: The longer you refrigerate the dough, the flakier the *parantha*. However do not refrigerate the dough for more than eight hours.

Tandoori Pyaaz Kulche

Dough

2 cups refined flour
½ teaspoon baking powder
¼ teaspoon soda bicarbonate
½ teaspoon salt
1 teaspoon sugar
½ cup milk
1 tablespoon yogurt
6 tablespoons oil
1½ tablespoons melted ghee

Stuffing

2 medium onions, chopped
2 green chillies, chopped
2 tablespoons chopped fresh coriander
Salt to taste
1 teaspoon caraway seeds

- Sift the flour together with the baking powder, soda bicarbonate and salt. Add the sugar, milk, yogurt and some water. Knead well into a medium-soft dough.
- Brush some oil on the dough, cover with a damp cloth and set aside for one hour.
- Divide the dough into four equal portions and shape into balls. For the filling, place the onions in a bowl.

Roti-Paranthe

- Add the green chillies, coriander, salt and caraway seeds, and mix well.
- Place the dough balls on a lightly floured surface and flatten slightly.
- Place a portion of the onion stuffing in the centre of each one, gather the edges together and seal. Cover with a damp cloth and rest for five minutes.
- Flatten each ball between your palms and roll into a nine-inch disc.
- Heat a pressure cooker, stick the *kulcha* onto the inside wall, and place the pressure cooker upside down over the gas flame.
- Cook for two to three minutes. You can also bake the *kulche* in a moderately hot *tandoor* for two to three minutes.
- Remove, brush with melted ghee and serve hot.

Paneer Aur Chawal Paranthe

1½ cups wholewheat flour
½ cup refined flour
Salt to taste
2 tablespoons ghee + for shallow-frying
¼ cup yogurt, whisked + to serve

Stuffing

¾ cup cooked rice, lightly mashed
¾ cup grated cottage cheese
1 medium onion, chopped
Salt to taste
3 green chillies, chopped
½ teaspoon red chilli powder
¼ teaspoon turmeric powder
½ teaspoon carom seeds
1 tablespoon chopped fresh coriander

- Sift together the wholewheat flour, refined flour and salt.
- Add two tablespoons of warm ghee and yogurt, and knead with enough water to make a soft dough. Cover with a damp cloth and set aside for half an hour.
- For the stuffing, mix together the rice, cottage cheese, onion, salt, green chillies, chilli powder, turmeric powder, carom seeds and chopped coriander in a large bowl. Divide into eight equal portions.

- Knead the dough again and divide into eight equal portions. Shape into balls and press between the palms of your hand.
- Roll out each ball into four-inch round and thin down the edges.
- Place a portion of the stuffing in the centre, gather the edges together and shape into a ball again.
- Roll out into a seven-inch round with a rolling pin.
- Heat a non-stick *tawa*. Place each *parantha* on it, turn it over once and drizzle a little melted ghee around it. Turn it over again and spread a little more ghee on the other side. Cook till both sides are well cooked.
- Serve hot with fresh yogurt and pickle.

Tandoori Roti

2 cups refined flour

Salt to taste

- Sift the flour and salt into a bowl.
- Add enough water and knead into a soft, smooth dough.
- Cover with a damp cloth and set aside for a few minutes. Divide the dough into four equal portions.
- Pat each ball on the palm of your hand, till approximately five or six-inch in diameter.
- Stick it onto the inner wall of a moderately hot *tandoor*. Remove when cooked. Serve hot.
- Alternatively, cook the *tandoori roti* in an oven. Place the *roti* on a greased baking tray and cook for five to six minutes at 190°C/375°F/Gas Mark 5.

Teekhat Meethachi Puri

2 teaspoons red chilli powder

Salt to taste

1 cup wholewheat flour

3 tablespoons semolina

½ teaspoon turmeric powder

1 teaspoon carom seeds

2 tablespoons oil + for deep-frying

- Sift together the flour and salt.
- Add the semolina, chilli powder, turmeric powder, carom seeds and two tablespoons of oil, and mix well.
- Add water, a little at a time and knead into a medium hard dough. Cover with a damp cloth for half an hour.
- Divide the dough into twelve to sixteen equal portions. Shape each portion into a ball and roll out into a three to four-inch *puri*.
- Heat the oil in a non-stick *kadai* and deep-fry the *puri* on both sides till puffed up and light golden brown.
- Drain on absorbent paper.
- Serve immediately.

Chef's Tip: These *puri* can be eaten as an evening snack with pickle, or served as an accompaniment to a main course.

Missi Roti

- 2 cups gram flour
- ¾ cup wholewheat flour
- ¼ cup chopped fresh coriander
- 4 green chillies, chopped
- 1 medium onion, chopped
- 1 teaspoon turmeric powder
- Salt to taste
- 1 teaspoon *chaat masala*
- 1 tablespoon dried pomegranate seeds
- 1 tablespoon oil + for greasing
- Butter, as required

- Sift together the gram flour and wholewheat flour into a bowl. Add the fresh coriander, green chillies, onion, turmeric powder, salt, *chaat masala*, dried pomegranate seeds and one tablespoon of oil.
- Add enough water to make a soft dough. Cover the dough with a damp cloth and rest it for ten minutes.
- Divide the dough into sixteen equal portions and shape into balls.
- Grease your palms with a little oil. Pat each ball of dough between your palms to make a six-inch round *roti*.
- Alternatively, roll out each ball on a greased and lightly floured surface.

- Heat a *tandoor*. Sprinkle water on one side of the *roti* and stick it onto the inner wall of the *tandoor*.

- Alternatively, cook the *roti* on a hot non-stick *tawa* till done. Spread with butter and serve hot.

Naan

- 4 cups refined flour
- 1 teaspoon baking powder
- ½ teaspoon soda bicarbonate
- 1 teaspoon salt
- 2 teaspoons sugar
- 1 cup milk
- 2 tablespoons yogurt
- 2 teaspoons onion seeds
- 12 tablespoons oil
- 2 teaspoons butter

- Sift the flour together with baking powder, soda bicarbonate and salt.
- Add the sugar, milk, yogurt and water. Knead well into a medium soft dough.
- Apply a little oil on the dough, cover with a damp cloth and set aside for one hour.
- Divide the dough into eight equal portions and shape into balls.
- Apply a little oil on each ball and sprinkle the onion seeds on top.
- Flatten each ball of dough into a six-inch circle.
- Stretch the dough on one side to make a triangular shape.
- Place on a piece of cloth and press onto the wall of a pre-heated *tandoor* or cook

in a preheated oven at 200°C/400°F/ Gas Mark 6.
- Remove with the help of skewers when crisp and brown on both sides.
- Serve hot, topped with butter.

Pudina Paranthe

2 cups wholewheat flour

10-12 sprigs fresh mint leaves

Salt to taste

Oil for shallow-frying

3 tablespoons butter

2 teaspoons *chaat masala*

- Wash and pat the mint leaves dry. Lightly roast half the leaves on a hot non-stick *tawa*. Cool and crush to a powder. Chop the remaining mint leaves.
- Place the flour and salt in a bowl. Add the chopped mint leaves and knead with enough water to make a stiff dough.
- Cover and rest the dough for twenty to twenty-five minutes.
- Divide the dough into six equal portions and shape into balls.
- Roll out each ball into a medium-sized *chapati*; brush with butter and sprinkle with some flour.
- Fold the *chapati* like a fan and twist it back into the shape of a ball. Leave to rest for five minutes.
- Roll out each ball into a five to seven-inch *parantha*.
- Cook on a hot non-stick *tawa*, brushing with a little oil on both sides, till light golden brown.

- Spread with butter while still hot.
- Mix the roasted mint powder and *chaat masala* together and sprinkle over the hot *paranthe*.
- Before serving, crush the *paranthe* lightly between your palms to open out the layers.

Chef's Tip: If you are using a *tandoor*, apply a little water on the side of the *parantha* that you are going to stick to the *tandoor* wall.

Rajasthani Baati

2 cups wholewheat flour
¼ teaspoon baking powder
2 teaspoons salt
⅔ cup pure ghee + for soaking
½ teaspoon carom seeds

- Sift the flour, baking powder and salt together. Rub two-third cup of ghee into the flour with your finger tips mixture till it resembles breadcrumbs.
- Add the carom seeds and approximately three-fourth cup of water and knead into a dough.
- Preheat an oven to 220°C/425°F/Gas Mark 7.
- Divide the dough into eight equal portions and shape into balls. Bake for about ten minutes.
- Lower heat to 200°C/400°F/Gas Mark 6 and continue to bake for thirty to thirty-five minutes longer.
- Remove from the oven, press lightly and soak in a bowl of melted ghee for at least one hour or till ready to serve.
- Serve with *dal* and ghee.

Glossary

English	Hindi	English	Hindi
Almonds	Badam	Mango, unripe, green	Keri
Asafoetida	Hing	Millet	Bajra
Barley	Jau	Mint, fresh	Pudina
Bengal gram, split	Chana dal	Olive	Jaitun
Caraway seeds	Shahi jeera	Onion seeds	Kalonji
Carom seeds	Ajwain	Radish	Mooli
Coriander seeds	Dhania	Raisins	Kishmish
Cornmeal	Makai ka atta	Red kidney beans	Rajma
Cottage cheese	Paneer	Refined flour	Maida
Cracked wheat	Dalia	Saffron	Kesar
Cumin seeds	Jeera	Screw pine	Kewra
Dried mango powder	Amchur	Semolina	Sooji/rawa
Dried pomegranate seeds	Anardana	Sesame seeds	Til
Fennel seeds	Badi Saunf	Sorghum	Jowar
Fenugreek leaves	Methi	Sweetcorn kernels	Makai ke dane
Fenugreek seeds	Methi dana	Turmeric	Haldi
Garlic, fresh, green	Lehsun ke taaze hare pattiyan	Wholewheat flour	Atta
Gram flour	Besan	Yeast	Khameer
Green gram, skinless split	Dhuli moong dal	Yogurt	Dahi